*Living*
## The Christian Life

# Living
# The Christian Life

*Are You Ready For A Supernatural and Spiritual Life with Jesus?*

> **Warning: This book could change your life! This change is forever!**

## John F. Hunter

Pastor evangelist
Chaplain missionary

| Library of Congress Control Number: | | 2015901050 |
| --- | --- | --- |
| ISBN: | Hardcover | 978-1-5035-3706-4 |
| | Softcover | 978-1-5035-3707-1 |
| | eBook | 978-1-5035-3708-8 |

Scripture quotations marked KJV are from the Holy Bible, King James Version (Authorized Version). First published in 1611. Quoted from the KJV Classic Reference Bible, Copyright © 1983 by The Zondervan Corporation

Print information available on the last page.

Rev. date: 02/10/2015

**To order additional copies of this book, contact:**
Xlibris
1-888-795-4274
www.Xlibris.com
Orders@Xlibris.com
637863

# CONTENTS

Chapter One. Am I In or Out?......................................7

Chapter Two. The Next Step.........................14

Chapter Three. The Second Ordinance............................18

Chapter Four. Supernatural Power! .............................22

Chapter Five. A New Life!............................................31

Chapter Six. Talking With God!.............................36

Chapter Seven. God's Family! ...................................41

Chapter Eight. God Speaks!.......................................48

Chapter Nine. Ambassadors for Christ ..........................57

Chapter Ten. In His Presence!.....................................62

Chapter Eleven. Your Mission ....................................65

Chapter Twelve. Alone with God .................................68

Chapter Thirteen. Exercise Faith................................82

# CHAPTER ONE

## Am I In or Out?

### The Place to Start

Am I in or out? Am I a Christian or not? What is a Christian? In 1970, I served as a US Army Chaplain's Assistant in Vietnam. While studying the Bible in the MAC-V (Fifth Military Airlift Command) Annex Chapel just outside of Saigon, several army and air force personnel tried to come up with the purest, simplest, and most accurate description of what a Christian is. I have not seen or heard a better or more accurate definition since that time. A true "Christian" is a person who has a personal relationship with the person of Jesus Christ.

Before we can live the Christian Life, there are some things we must understand. First of all, *living* the Christian Life is not a list of things to do or things not to do. Instead, it is a supernatural life with Jesus living in you. This is a serious decision that each one of us must choose for our self to accept or reject.

Regardless of who you are, God loves you and can give you eternal life; you can live forever! God's words in the Bible give us a set of Christian principles to live by. With these principles, you can make the right choices and decisions throughout your life. Living the Christian Life is not a philosophy or just a good way to live. Instead, living the Christian life is living within the supernatural power of God, the giver of all life. The only way a person can live the Christian life is with the supernatural help of God.

You have to first become a Christian before you can start living the Christian life. The good news is that if you are not a Christian, you have choices: you can choose to become a Christian, or you can choose to simply learn about who Christians are and what they believe. So are you in or are you out?

If you are a Christian, how long have you been one? Do you understand the work God is calling you to do? If you are truly a Christian, then you are said to be "saved." All who are saved are called by God to a special mission in the greatest operation in history, but first we need to review our understanding of salvation and our responsibility to share the Good News with others. If you are not a Christian, do you want to be a Christian? The question is not so much "am I in or out?" but really "do I *want* to be in or not?" You got to make that choice!

If God made you, then it is He alone who knows why; and He alone has the authority and power to give you purpose, meaning, hope, and direction for your life.

A person is not saved by getting all excited and shouting. A person is not saved by being baptized. God's own words in the Bible show us the only way of salvation that God has provided for us. A person knows for sure if they are saved by seeing if they are in compliance with God's plan for salvation. Holy God, who made us, is the only one qualified to make the rules! We can decide to believe and accept His generous offer, but His way is the only way there is because He is the only true God there is! He made the earth, sun, moon, and stars and gave all living creatures their existence.

We, Christians, believe God used spiritual men in the past to write down for us all of His truth in His own words, the Bible. God tells us in the Bible all we need to know about living the Christian Life and how to know if we are in or out.

**Luke 4:4 And Jesus answered him, saying, "It is written, that man shall not live by bread alone, but by every word of God."**

**Matt. 4:4 But he answered and said, "It is written, Man shall not live by bread alone, but by every word that proceedeth out of the mouth of God."**

Because all of us have sinned, we need to be saved or redeemed. Do you know anyone who is perfect? Of course not! God and heaven are all that is perfect, pure, and holy. God is completely pure and right. God will not allow anything or anyone contaminated with the rot and stink of sin to enter into His presence.

When an apple is rotten, do you keep it with the good apples? No! You throw it away so it doesn't contaminate the entire basket of good apples. Bad apples will contaminate the good apples, and they will all rot. Sin is anything you do that you know is morally or ethically wrong. Anything we do that is not right in God's eyes separates us from the right-ness of God. That's why mankind must be thrown away. But God loves us and has provided a way for us to be restored or redeemed from our rotten sin and for us to come into fellowship with God, who loves us.

In order for us to enter heaven, we must be pure and holy in the presence of God. All people on the earth have sinned against God, and the wage of sin is death. But God is not willing to just let us all be thrown away into the fires of Hell. That's why God came to be with men on earth in the human form of Jesus to pay our debt Himself with His own suffering and with His own blood and to die in our place.

He came to redeem us from the rot and stink of sin and to restore us to fellowship with God. God, who made us to begin with, is the giver of all life; but the contamination of sin removes us from God's gift of life. God's words say in the books of Romans and Galatians:

**Rom. 3:23 For all have sinned, and come short of the glory of God.**

> **Rom. 6:23 For the wages of sin is death; but the gift of God is eternal Life through Jesus Christ our Lord.**

> **Gal. 3:13 Christ hath redeemed us from the curse of the law, being made a curse for us: for it is written, Cursed is every one that hangeth on a tree.**

Jesus is God revealing Himself to us in the form of a man. Jesus came to earth born of a virgin and without an earthly father because He is the seed of God, not of a man. He became completely human to experience human temptation, pain, and suffering.

Jesus, being God in the form of a man, was able to resist temptation and had no sin. He also was able to feel all of the pain, hunger, love, and desire that we experience. He was able to suffer and die in our place to pay for our sins. As our scapegoat, He became the blood sacrifice for all of the wrong we ever did. The result of sin is death, and that means death forever and ever in the fires of hell; but Jesus paid our debt by His death because He made us and loves us.

God's divine love and forgiveness are not found in any other religious beliefs. Jesus rose from death to life again to prove that He has power and authority over death. He has the power to give life forever to anyone who is truly sorry for their sins and wants to do what is right.

We cannot do what is right by ourselves. We cannot save ourselves; but the blood of Christ covers our sins, and we appear as perfect in the sight of God.

> **Rom. 5:8 But God commandeth His love toward us, in that, while we were yet sinners, Christ died for us.**

**John 3:16 For God so loved the world, that He gave His only begotten Son, that whosoever believeth in Him should not perish, but have everlasting life.**

In the book of First Corinthians, Paul says to us:

**1 Cor. 15:1–4 Moreover, brethren, I declare unto you the gospel which I preached unto you, which also ye have received, and wherein ye stand; By which also ye are saved, if ye keep in memory what I preached unto you, unless ye have believed in vain. For I delivered unto you first of all that which I also received, how that Christ died for our sins according to the scriptures; And that He was buried, and that He rose again the third day according to the scriptures.**

The Grace of God is that we get what we do not deserve and cannot earn. God provides Eternal Life to us as a free gift. Jesus has already paid the price and has purchased our salvation with His own blood and suffering. Jesus Christ has already done all that can be done to purchase our pardon. All we can do is accept Jesus as Savior and give ourselves to Him. We must make the choice to accept or reject the free gift He offers to us. This gift of Eternal Life cost Jesus plenty; it was very expensive and is very valuable, but Jesus has already paid for it and we cannot. If we accept Jesus as our Savior, Lord, and Master, He gives us power to become His children. He wants us to live for Him, and He wants what is best for us. God has a beautiful plan for your life!

We must repent our sins, accept Jesus as savior, and seek to do God's will for our life. He wants our total faith and commitment to obey Him. Only when we give Him our full and complete trust and control of our life can He give us the peace in our hearts and joyful meaning, hope, direction, and purpose that we all need in order to be fulfilled and happy children of the living God.

> **Eph. 2:8–9 For by grace are ye saved through faith; and that not of yourselves: it is the gift of God: Not of works, lest any man should boast.**

It is important that we make a public confession that Jesus is our Savior. That is why the church invites us to come up front and to tell the people that we accept Jesus as Savior. You will know for sure you are saved because you know for sure how the Bible, the Word of God, says we are saved.

Only when you are saved are you *in* instead of *out*. A person cannot live the Christian life until that person has believed and has given his or her heart to God. Once saved, that person is spiritually changed forever! Now that we know the truth, we have a responsibility to tell others about the Good News of the gospel of salvation.

Wouldn't it be awful if we knew someone was asleep in a burning building, and we didn't even try to wake them up or to get them out? We must warn others that without Jesus, they have no hope of salvation and living forever.

> **Rom. 10:9–11 That if thou shalt confess with your thy mouth the Lord Jesus, and shalt believe in thine heart that God hath raised Him from the dead, thou shalt be saved. For with**

**the heart man believeth
unto righteousness; and
with the mouth confession
is made unto salvation.
For the scripture saith,
Whosoever believeth on
Him shall not be ashamed.**

Only God knows exactly what position and job He is calling you to do; but first there will be a time of training, learning, and preparation. The first step in living the Christian Life is to be Saved. But Jesus, who is fully man and also fully God, says there is only one way to be saved and to go to heaven:

**John 14:6 Jesus saith unto him, "I am
the way, the truth, and the
life: no man cometh unto
the Father, but by me."**

So there is no other way to eternal life with God because God says so; and only God, the creator, gets to make the rules!

# Chapter Two

## The Next Step

### Baptism and Church Membership

Once a person knows if they are in or out, that means you know what Salvation is and whether you are "saved" or not. The first step is Salvation, and the next step is Baptism and Church membership.

The next step for a new Christian, after accepting Jesus Christ as savior and making a public confession in front of the church, is to be baptized. Baptism does not wash away your sins and does not help save you. The blood of Christ Jesus washes away your sins. Believing in the Lord Jesus Christ as your savior with all of your heart is what saves you.

Baptism is a public testimony of your new life in Christ. We need to be baptized to show our love and obedience to Jesus, who set the example by being baptized Himself and commands us to baptize all new believers after they are saved. This is a dramatic opportunity to act out your faith for all to see. Maybe others will ask questions and be saved after seeing you being baptized.

> **Mark 1:9 And it came to pass in those days, that Jesus came from Nazareth of Galilee, and was baptized of John in Jordan.**

Baptism signifies the death, burial, and resurrection of Christ. Your being completely immersed below the surface of the water also signifies the death of your sinful old self as it is likened to being dead and buried in a grave; and your being raised up from the water signifies your new life with Christ. As a new person, you are also looking forward to the time you leave this earth; and your body will be buried in the grave, but your spirit will rise to live forever with God in heaven.

This is why many churches, such as Baptist churches, baptize only by total immersion, to signify death, burial, and resurrection to new life. Baptists believe that pouring water on someone or sprinkling does not truly demonstrate the death, burial, and raising up from the grave.

Churches trying to follow New Testament Bible examples point out that immersion seems to be the method of baptism demonstrated by Jesus and His followers (followers are called disciples) because people always meet at the river or the sea or a body of water. Also, all examples of baptism in the Bible describe the people going down into the water to be baptized and coming up out of the water. See what God's Word says:

**Col. 2:12 Buried with Him in baptism, wherein also ye are risen with Him through the faith of the operation of God, who hath raised Him from the dead.**

**Acts 8:38–39 And he commanded the chariot to stand still: and they went down both into the water, both Philip and the eunuch; and he baptized him. And when they were come up out of the water, the Spirit of the Lord caught away Philip, that the eunuch saw him no more: and he went on his way rejoicing.**

> **Mark 1:9–11 And it came to pass in those days, that Jesus came from Nazareth of Galilee, and was baptized of John in Jordan. And straightway coming up out of the water, He saw the heavens opened, and the Spirit like a dove descending upon Him: And there came a voice from heaven, saying, "Thou art my beloved Son, in whom I am well pleased."**

Although baptism does not save you, it is unlikely that a truly saved person would want to go very long after being saved without wanting to be baptized in order to fulfill all that is right and expected as instructed by God's word, the Bible. Baptism is the first ordinance administered by the church to a new Christian.

> **Matt. 28:18–20 And Jesus came and spake unto them, saying, "All power is given unto me in heaven and in earth." Go ye therefore, and teach all nations, baptizing them in the name of the Father, and of the Son, and of the Holy Ghost: Teaching them to observe all things whatsoever I have commanded you: and, lo, I am with you always, even unto the end of the world. Amen."**

Because Jesus commanded us to do it, established it as a requirement, and expected us to do it, we refer to Baptism as the first ordinance completed for a new Christian joining a local church congregation. A true Christian should want to be baptized soon after being saved thereby accepting Jesus the Christ as his/her personal Savior, Lord, and Master.

I still remember accepting Jesus as my Savior at seven years old and walking down in front of the church to make my personal confession of Jesus Christ as Savior, Lord, and Master on Easter morning in 1958, in the First Baptist Church of New Franklin, Missouri, where we lived. I also remember attending a youth group in the basement of the church a few weeks later and being very frustrated. The youth were playing games and eating refreshments. Although the youth and their leaders did pray and give a devotional before eating, I was disappointed because I came to search for God's calling and for direction in my life!

My father was a pastor at this time in a small rural church near Fayette, Missouri, and I got to be baptized by my earthly father in a lake near New Franklin. I still remember some small fish were swimming around my leg, and some cattle were standing in the water on the other side of the lake. We worshiped God in the name of Jesus and prayed. Salvation and the meaning of baptism were explained. I confessed again that I had accepted Jesus as my savior and Lord before being baptized completely under the water and, of course, rising back up out of the water to complete the picture of a "watery grave" and resurrection to a new life with Christ.

A Christian is a follower of Jesus, who is referred to in the Bible as Jesus Christ. Jesus is the English translation of Yeshua, and "Christ" is translated to mean "the Savior" or "the Messiah," so this is where the word Christian came from. Baptism is part of beginning to live the supernatural and spiritual life I call living the Christian Life.

# CHAPTER THREE

## The Second Ordinance

### The Next Step

The next step for a Christian—after accepting Jesus as Savior, making a public confession in front of the church, and being baptized—is to take part in the Lord's Supper. This is the second ordinance administered by the church to a new Christian. We are commanded by Jesus to observe the Lord's Supper in remembrance of His body being sacrificed and His life-giving blood being given for us when He suffered and died in our place on the cross.

Although Baptism is usually considered a one–time special event for a new believer, Jesus established the communion (or Lord's Supper) to be a repeated ceremony to help us remember His body and blood being given to fulfill our redemption and Salvation on the cross. That is why Baptism is referred to as the first ordinance, and the Lord's Supper as the second ordinance. He did not tell us how often to do it.

> **1 Cor. 11:23–26 For I have received of the Lord that which also I delivered unto you, that the Lord Jesus the same night in which He was betrayed took bread: And when He had**

**given thanks, He brake it, and said "Take, eat: this is my body, which is broken for you: this do in remembrance of me." After the same manner also He took the cup, when He had supped, saying, "This cup is the new testament in my blood: this do ye, as oft as ye drink it, in remembrance of me." For as often as ye eat this bread, and drink this cup, ye do shew the Lord's death till He come.**

Because the Lord did not specify how often to observe the Lord's Supper, different churches administer the Lord's Supper at different times. Some churches do it every Sunday as a part of the worship service. Some do it once a month, once a quarter, or even once a year. Some include observance of the Lord's Supper as part of a special service or on certain important holidays.

A local Christian church is a congregation of Christians meeting together for worship, fellowship, learning, encouragement, and support of each other in living the Christian Life. The local church congregation administers the ordinances of Baptism and the Lord's Supper to those who have joined themselves to the local family of God.

Some church families only extend the invitation to members of their own local church family. They may call this "closed Communion." Some local church families extend the invitation to include all visitors who are also saved, born again Christian believers.

God gives us stern warnings about not taking the Lord's Supper unworthily!

**1 Cor. 11:27–31 Wherefore whosoever shall eat this bread, and drink this cup of the Lord,**

**unworthily, shall be guilty of the body and blood of the Lord. But let a man examine himself, and so let him eat of that bread, and drink of that cup. For he that eateth and drinketh unworthily, eateth and drinketh damnation to himself, not discerning the Lord's body. For this cause many are weak and sickly among you, and many sleep. For if we would judge ourselves, we should not be judged.**

If you feel your heart is not right with God, it is better to wait until you get that taken care of first.

In the same local community, there may be many church congregations with different names. Some may call themselves Catholic, some Baptist, some Presbyterians, and some Nazarenes. There are many groups that call themselves Christians but may not all agree on all beliefs or teachings.

The building where churches meet is often called a church, but the meeting place is not the church. The local church is the group of believers called the "congregation or "body of believers, regardless of where they meet. When you attend any of these churches, be sure to look for one that you believe teaches the Bible correctly.

I have very fond memories of the Rising Sun Baptist Church, way out in the country, 18 miles from the nearest town. I remember in the 1980s and 1990s, we would celebrate the Lord's Supper communion by candlelight on Thursday evenings before Easter Sunday. The only light in the room was that coming from the candles. Everyone would sit very quietly and prayerfully as the pastor, reading by candlelight, presented how Jesus broke the bread and passed the cup at the end of the Jewish feast of Passover.

The tables were arranged in the shape of a cross, and even the children were very still and respectful as they understood that this was a very serious and spiritual ceremony to help us remember Jesus giving his body and blood as He died on the cross. This was a special time to show our reverence for Jesus and the seriousness of His suffering and sacrifice for us. Easter Sunday was always the day we observed the resurrection of Jesus from the grave.

# CHAPTER FOUR

## Supernatural Power!

### Beyond the Laws of Physics and Nature

God is the creator of all that exists. The true and real God is the Lord, owner and King of everything, including all of the major events in history! He is not some image or idol made with human hands and placed on a wall to burn incense and pray to! God is not a statue made of gold by men to be worshiped! God is the one and only real true God.

We did not make God out of our fears, wants, needs, and imaginations; he is the one who made us! He is the only source of life, power, and authority. God created the universe so vast that no powerful telescope has ever seen to the other side of it. God made the universe, the earth, the sun, the moon, and the stars. He is to be feared, worshiped, and served; and he is firmly in control of all world events throughout history!

This is a mystery, but it is one which is not that hard to understand. God is everywhere—in all places and at all times! God is able to come to us in the form of a man. He is able to send us a messenger or angel. God has the power to allow us to sometimes see the angels! Science, nature, and evolution did not make God; God made science, nature, and physics! God is not limited by the laws of science and nature because He is the one who made and created the laws of science, nature, and physics. He created and has complete control over the laws of physics and science, which control the things we can see and touch. They obey His every will and command!

God does not have to fit into what we understand! Instead of fitting into what we think is possible, all reality, science, nature, and the laws of physics must obey and fit into the creator's will and control! A true Christian must live in the supernatural power of God.

> **Gen. 1:1–2 In the beginning God created the heaven and the earth. And the earth was without form, and void; and darkness was upon the face of the deep. And the Spirit of God moved upon the face of the waters.**

Long ago, long before there were people or dinosaurs, there was God. And way back before there was time or space as we know it, God was creating and giving life in the Spiritual realm. He made angels, cherubim, and seraphim. God always was, always is, and always will be; and we are not able to comprehend it. We cannot fully understand it because all we know and understand is not the spirit world until the Spirit of God in us reveals it to us. All we know and understand in our limited human experience has a beginning somewhere in time and space. We have no experience or memory of forever past or forever future.

God, who always was and always is and always will be, made angels, cherubim, and seraphim in another spiritual realm; but we were not yet; then God made us too. And God came to walk on the earth with men in the form of the man Jesus, and God used wise men of old to write it all down for us in His own words the Bible. Jesus did not begin when he was born as a baby from a virgin woman; Jesus (also called "Yeshua in the old original languages) was already with God and was not fully separate from God when heaven and earth were created. Jesus is also referred to in the Book of John as the Word, and Jesus was the part of God that created heaven and earth in chapter 1 of the book of Genesis.

**John 1:1–3 In the beginning was the Word, and the Word was with God, and the Word was God. The same was in the beginning with God. All things were made by him; and without Him was not any thing made that was made.**

This is a mystery beyond our full comprehension. Although God's words in the Bible teach us about God the Father, God the Son, and God the Spirit, there is only one God. The Father, Jesus, and the Spirit are all integrated into one God, and He is the only true God there is. He is the only one that created heaven and earth. God is the only God that made mankind. All other gods are just idols or great people in history. Only God is the Lord.

Much like the hub, spokes, and rim are all part of a wheel; but none of the parts are a wheel by themselves. Although Jesus is God, there is also a Father and a Holy Spirit; but Jesus is often called the Son of God because there is a father, and sometimes called the Son of man, as He was also able to be born of flesh through the virgin girl. John 1:14 continues to explain:

**John 1:14 And the Word was made flesh, and dwelt among us, (and we beheld His glory, the glory as of the only begotten of the Father,) full of grace and truth.**

Jesus lives in Father God and in God's Holy Spirit. Almighty God the Father lives in Jesus, the Son, and in the Holy Spirit. The Holy Spirit of God lives in Jesus and also in the Father. God is all three, and they are one God. Any person who denies miracles in their life is also denying his or her own birth, which would appear impossible! The changes a caterpillar goes through also seem impossible, but it changes into a beautiful butterfly! A person cannot call himself/herself a Christian and deny living in the supernatural. During His life as a human here on earth, Jesus worked many miracles of love, compassion, and good. He healed the sick, made the blind see, made the crippled walk, and casted out evil spirits; then, He instructed His followers before He rose miraculously up into the heavens that anyone who believes in Him would do "greater things than these"! Listen to Jesus's own words in chapter 14 of John.

> **John 14:12–14 "Verily, Verily, I say unto you, he that believeth on me, the works that I do shall he do also; and greater works than these shall he do; because I go unto my Father. And whatsoever ye shall ask in my name, that will I do, that the Father may be glorified in the Son. If ye shall ask any thing in my name, I will do it . . ."**

Strong faith leads to supernatural power! Jesus told His disciples (or followers) that if they would ask anything in His name, He would do it! But that's not all. Jesus pointed out the great miracles he had performed and went on to say that if they would put their faith in Him and ask in His name, the disciples would do even greater things than He himself had done! According to God's word, the Bible, we can become the sons of God and Jesus' disciples and receive power!

> **Acts 1:8 "But ye shall receive power, after that the Holy Ghost is come upon you: and ye shall be witnesses unto me both in Jerusalem, and in all Judaea, and in Samaria, and unto the uttermost part of the earth."**

God, who made us, also gave us great value. We are very valuable to God. God didn't have to love us, but He chose to love us and to give us great value. Our minds have no history of forever, and we have no experience or understanding of forever past.

We are like a flower that has no awareness of its own value to the owner because its life form is so different from the owner. We are so helpless without the power and love of God.

If you are truly saved and born again spiritually, you are a new creature; old things are passed away, and all things are made new. If you are truly saved, the Holy Spirit of the living God is even now changing the way you think; and you are becoming more loving, more forgiving, more compassionate, and more in-tune with God.

Pray every day for God to help you love, serve, and worship Him better. Pray for God to help you love others, and pray that He will use you to help others. These changes are forever! God's Spirit changes the way you think about things in your brain and the way you feel about things in your heart.

You will never be the same again if you are a true Christian. This is part of your everlasting new life with the supernatural Jesus. Your body actually becomes the temple of the Living God as Jesus now lives in you.

> **John 14:16–20 "And I will pray the Father, and He shall give you another Comforter, that He may abide with you for ever; Even the Spirit of truth; whom the world cannot receive, because it seeth Him not, neither knoweth Him: but ye know Him; for He dwelleth with you, and shall be in you. I will not leave you comfortless: I will come to you. Yet a little while, and the world seeth me no more; but ye see me: because I live, ye**

**shall live also. At that day ye shall know that I am in my Father, and ye in me, and I in you . . ."**

**2 Cor. 5:17 Therefore if any man be in Christ, he is a new creature: old things are passed away; behold, all things are become new.**

I have experienced many supernatural events in my life that should not have been possible unless God was helping us. I remember during our first mission trip to Arizona that we were traveling into places that were far from home and that we had never been to.

I was driving the one-ton dual-wheel truck pulling our only home, a thirty-nine-and-a-half-foot RV mission trailer. The truck and Fifth Wheel trailer hooked together are fifty-three feet long and thirteen feet and four inches high. At that time, I had very little experience pulling an eleven-and-a-half-ton rig over the mountains. Sandy would drive our small economy car along behind the big rig so we would have a cheaper means of transportation when we arrive in Globe, Arizona.

We had been warned by more than one truck driver not to take a long, heavy rig through the Salt River Canyon, which we later drove through in the car. Let me tell you: the Salt River Canyon is so impressive that if you had never seen the Grand Canyon and if somebody told you it was the Grand Canyon, you would likely believe it!

So we planned a southern route through Las Cruces, New Mexico, to get on Interstate highway I-10. We started out on the 1,450-mile trip with little more than our faith in the supernatural power of God because we believed that was what God was leading us to do. We drove southwest on Highway 60 through Clovis, New Mexico, and Highway 70 through Roswell then up a huge mountain that strained the limits of our 1992 Black Silverado Chevy truck. We stopped near the top, where we could find room to pull off, to rest and let the truck rest as well.

Finally with our nerves somewhat recovered, we pushed on. It turned out that we were just around the bend from the downhill ascent into Las Cruces, New Mexico. As we rolled effortlessly down the mountainside into Las Cruces, which is Spanish for "The Crosses," I could hear the awful sound I dreaded.

Here we are—a thousand miles from home, in a strange place we have never been to, without friends or means of assistance, nobody to call for help (pretty much all alone), except for the God who said "I will never leave you nor forsake you." I could hear a rod banging loudly in the engine and knew the engine was ruined!

I backed the trailer into the lot behind the Pilot truck stop on highway I-10. I unhooked the truck from the trailer for the last time. I told Sandy "We have to pray. We can never hook this truck up to the mission trailer again. "We don't know what to do, but we know God has a plan!"

We were helpless without His help, so we prayed to God in the name of Jesus. We asked for wisdom, direction, and courage. We asked Him to show us what to do, and we proceeded across the street to another truck stop where there was a nice restaurant to get supper. We also needed to relax our weary bones and to calm our stressed-out nerves. We did a lot of praying that night.

Later I looked back on the incident and could see that God had planned out the entire situation; but right then, we had nothing but our faith in the loving, supernatural, and powerful God of the universe.

We weren't scared because we knew that God always has a plan! The situation looked serious and bad. Even though the old truck could still pull the heavy mission trailer just fine on flat ground, we were facing hundreds of miles through scorching desert and steep mountain passes. Notice that God did not allow us to break down way out in the wilderness, but He made sure it was in the city—where there are services, businesses, and people.

Once a person pulls out on I-10 going west, it could be over a hundred miles between fuel stations and convenience stores. Most pockets of civilization do not include any mechanical shops. The temperature in far Southern New Mexico and Arizona can be well over a hundred degrees! No sane person would start out with a truck with a banging rod and a huge load over twenty-three thousand pounds to drag hundreds of miles up countless steep mountains. We were less than twenty-five miles from the border of Mexico in places.

Fortunately we had our only home and everything we owned with us in the mission trailer so we could sleep in our own bed at night! We did a lot of praying to God in the name of Jesus and requested the Holy Spirit of God to give us courage, strength, and wisdom to know what to do. We put it all in God's hands and slept well. We fully trusted God to help us, but we had no idea what He would do or what we were going to do!

I don't know what caused us to take the old truck across the intersection diagonally to a tire place that does oil changes and tune-ups, but we paid seventy-five dollars for a full servicing. I came to believe it was a part of God's plan. It was there in the waiting room that we ran into a man who told us what to do next. I'm pretty sure he said his last name was Suggs, but I can't be certain what his first name was; and now I'm not sure if he was a mortal man or an angel sent to us by God. He told us he was in some kind of a septic tank business (or maybe it was portable toilet business). Anyway he said they got all of their heavy-duty trucks from the Car Store and were always treated right. He gave us simple directions on how to get there. He even gave us the name of the owner and his brother's name. He also said they would treat us right. So Sandy and I took the car and went to the Car Store.

It was plain to see that the "Car Store" didn't have a single car! The only thing the Car Store had was big heavy-hauling trucks and huge boats! All of the trucks were dual-rear wheel trucks, one-ton or bigger, with heavy-duty Cummins Diesel engines; and the boats were big yachts and cabin cruisers that would have to be hauled on large trailers. The only cars that were there were those of the customers and workers. Some of the trucks were red, some were blue, and most were white; and they were in a wide range of prices.

I called our banker back in Missouri and handed the phone to the owner of the Car Store. When they were done talking, which didn't take very long . . . Well, let's just say that two days after our arrival, we rolled out of town with a truck that was nine years newer, got twice as good fuel mileage and a whole lot more power; and we never put any money on the table—not even a penny! All they did was give us some trade-in on the black Chevrolet, moved the payments from the old truck to the new truck, and moved the payments from one bank to the other bank. Oh sure, we had to pay sales tax on the license when the temporary tag ran out sixty days later; but we were on our way.

I believe God planned the whole thing. I believe He wanted us to have newer, better, more dependable equipment and a powerful testimony to share. He also wanted us to exercise our faith, to make our faith grow stronger. By the way, neither the people at the Car Store nor anyone else seemed to know any man named Suggs, who had a septic tank or porta-potty business and knew everybody's name and phone numbers at the Car Store.

To this day, the white, one-ton Dodge Ram 3500 with 5.9-liters of Cummins turbo-Diesel has proven to be very dependable in pulling an eleven-ton rig across the countryside. Since then, we have been to Arizona (twenty-nine hundred miles round trip) from Missouri and down to Georgia (fifteen hundred miles round trip) several times and many other missions in and around the state of Missouri with the same 5.9 liters of Cummins Diesel.

# CHAPTER FIVE

*A New Life!*

## Growing Spiritually with Christ

Living the Christian Life is such an exciting journey! If you are in—that is if you are truly saved and have accepted Jesus as Savior, Lord, and Master—then God is changing you right now! When you are saved and have become a true, supernatural Christian, you become a new person and will never be the same again. Now Jesus lives in your heart through the Holy Spirit of God. If you are truly saved, you are continually becoming more Christ-like.

How much you grow spiritually and how fast you mature are up to you. Once a baby is born, he or she begins a new life. When a person accepts Jesus Christ as savior, he or she becomes a "Christian." They also begin an exciting, new life. When our old self dies and we are raised to new life in Christ, we are said to be "Born Again." At the very moment you open your heart to accept Jesus as Savior, the Holy Spirit of God enters you; and you become a new creature.

A newly born Christian is not a mature Christian. Just like a newborn baby, a new baby Christian has to be fed, has much to learn, and must be nurtured. Often the words of God in the Bible are referred to as "spiritual food."

**2 Cor. 5:17 Therefore if any man be in Christ, he is a new creature: old things are passed away; behold, all things are become new.**

**John 3:6–7 "That which is born of the flesh is flesh; and that which is born of the Spirit is spirit. Marvel not that I said unto thee, Ye must be born again . . ."**

There are six basic ways in which a Christian grows to spiritual maturity (you can count them using five fingers on your one hand and a thumb on the other or your big toe to help you remember). That's right! There are six basic ways you can grow into a strong and healthy Christian. Without these six activities, you cannot become a healthy and mature Christian:

1) Prayer (talking with God in the name of Jesus)
2) Fellowship (sharing with other Christians)
3) Bible Study (learning from God's Word)
4) Witnessing (telling others about Jesus)
5) Worship (praising & glorifying God in Jesus' name)
6) Giving (giving of yourself for the needs of others)

**1 Cor. 3:1–2 And I, brethren, could not speak unto you as unto spiritual, but as unto carnal, even as unto babes in Christ. I have fed you with milk, and not with meat: for hitherto ye were not able to bear it, neither yet now are ye able.**

Living the Christian Life requires a lifetime of training, experience, and learning. Spiritual growth is a process of preparation to live in the supernatural.

Sometimes God is preparing, training, teaching, and mentoring us to be ready for the work we are going to do in the future; and we aren't even aware of it until later. I was working as a licensed nurse at the Maximum Security facility of Missouri Department of Mental Health in Fulton, Missouri, when I received a very interesting phone call.

Several people who did not know each other had said to me over several months that Fulton Reception and Diagnostic Center (FRDC)—just up the street from the Biggs Building in Fulton State Hospital, where I was working—was looking for a chaplain, and they thought I should apply for the position. They all seemed to agree, although none of them had ever spoken with each other, that I had just the qualifications they were looking for.

I was aware that the Department of Corrections and the Department of Mental Health were both a part of the same retirement system, but it never occurred to me that I would be qualified under state requirements as I knew the army required a master's degree in religion, ministry, or theology.

Up to this time, I also had never felt any calling from God to get involved in prison ministry, but could several unrelated people all be wrong? And this phone call was from a man I knew and respected as one who was dedicated to serving God in the name of Jesus. He would not have called unless he felt strongly that God's Spirit was urging him to call me with a very special message.

This man said "John, I don't think you understand. I truly believe God told me to call you." He repeated what several other people had told me: I needed to apply for the position of chaplain at FRDC, which is a receiving center for men entering the Missouri prison system.

After much prayer and meditation, I reasoned that I could apply and pray. This way the Department of Corrections would know who I was and could review my qualifications and experiences. At the same time, I reasoned that if I did not meet their requirements or if this was not God's will, I would never hear from them again. In other words, I did my part; and now the situation would be out of my hands and into God's.

You know, it is true that just prior to this time, I had been praying intensely about my future and the ministry. It is true that God had put it in my heart that I was not to accept any more jobs that were not related to ministry (not even to waste time trying to raise a garden). I knew God was going to move me out of the nursing job at Fulton State Hospital, but I had placed resumes to be the pastor of a local church. I had resumes in front of churches and associations in three different states and didn't get a single call! But I knew God had a plan. Well, things began to happen!

The Supervisor of Religious and Spiritual Services, (basically, the state's chief of chaplains) for the Department of Corrections asked me to interview for the chaplain position at Cameron, Missouri; then I was asked to interview for the chaplain position at Bowling Green, Missouri. Of course, I was not aware that the Associate Superintendent of Operations from FRDC was at both of those interviews; then I was asked a question.

I was asked "If the Department of Corrections were to hire you as a chaplain, would you prefer to serve at Cameron, Bowling Green, or Fulton?" My reply was simple enough: If I took the position at Fulton, I wouldn't have to move my family to another town. I was already working at Biggs, which is less than a city block's distance up the street. A few weeks later, I was told to begin my new job as the chaplain at FRDC on April 6, 1998.

I retired from my job at Mental Health and started a new one at the Department of Corrections, which is still the same retirement system. I was able to carry my eighteen years of retirement benefits with me to the new job and continue to add years to my retirement benefits. But then I got to thinking.

I began to realize that God was preparing me for this job all of my life—even back when I was only seven years old! I remembered standing behind my father's leg and listening to him tell others about how he would deal with the men. You see, my dad was the chaplain for the Missouri State Training School for Boys in Boonville in the 1950s. This same facility is today BCC (Boonville Correctional Center) and now has a prison fence around it.

I also remember attending Sunday school and church, teaching Sunday School, serving in the 1970s on the Correctional Services Missions of Missouri, serving as chaplain assistant in the US Army in

Vietnam and as the chaplain assistant supervisor for the Missouri Army National Guard. I was also the pastor of a small church in Molino, North of Mexico, Missouri, for several years. I was amazed at how God was working all those years to put me right where he wanted me, but I knew that God was using me as a tool to do His work.

I was aware that the success of the ministry at FRDC depended on Him, and I couldn't take any credit for it. If I had ever thought it was about me, I would have been of no use to Him; and He would have had to replace me. I did, however, feel a strong sense of satisfaction and fulfillment in knowing I was right where God wanted me to be. I am very thankful to God for allowing me to be a small part of His ministry.

Many men were able to change their lives from one of hopelessness, anger, frustration, and desperation to one of hope, meaning, purpose, and direction through Jesus Christ as a result of a very effective chapel ministry program.

# CHAPTER SIX

## Talking With God!

### Spending Time with Supernatural God

Talking with God in the name of Jesus is a vital part of living the Christian Life. As we begin the exciting new journey of our new life with Jesus Christ, we must spend some time with our Master, Lord, and King! God will spend time with us and speak to us, if we will listen. A Christian is a person who has a personal relationship with the person of Jesus Christ. We cannot build an intimate relationship with someone we love unless we spend some time with them!

As God's little children, God loves us. Father God is our spiritual Daddy, and He calls us His "little children. Even if we are physically grown or old, He still calls us "little children. Whether we are six years old or eighty years old, we need to grow spiritually every day. I have some friends that are ninety-three and one hundred years old, and God still sees them as His little children. When we talk with God, we can call it "prayer, but it is really just having a conversation with God in the name of Jesus. He is everywhere at all times, so we can talk to Him throughout the day.

**1 Thess. 5:17 Pray without ceasing.**

**James 5:16 Confess your faults one
to another, and pray one**

**for another, that ye may
be healed. The effectual
fervent prayer of a righteous
man availeth much.**

We can thank Jesus for loving us and for giving us eternal life. We can glorify God for His awesome grace, love, mercy, and forgiveness. We can ask for help in times of trouble, or we can ask Him to show us what to do. We can ask for guidance and wisdom in making important decisions, or we can ask for strength and courage to do the right thing.

We can pray for those who are lost, without any hope of salvation, that the Holy Spirit of God will convict them in their hearts that they need to be saved. It is wise right from the start to get into the habit of praying every day. Many Christians teach their children to pray every night when they get into bed; and some businessmen pray early in the morning before breakfast or with their morning coffee or tea. Always remember to pray in the name of Jesus (or Yeshua).

**Col. 3:17 And whatsoever ye do in
word or deed, do all in the
name of the Lord Jesus,
giving thanks to God and
the Father by Him.**

**John 14:13–14 "And whatsoever ye
shall ask in my name, that
will I do, that the Father
may be glorified in the
Son. If ye shall ask any
thing in my name, I will
do it . . ."**

**Phil. 2:8–11 And being found in
fashion as a man, He
humbled Himself, and
became obedient unto
death, even the death of
the cross. Wherefore God**

**also hath highly exalted Him, and given Him a name which is above every name: That at the name of Jesus every knee should bow, of things in heaven, and things in earth, and things under the earth; And that every tongue should confess that Jesus Christ is Lord, to the glory of God the Father.**

**Phil. 4:6 Be careful for nothing; but in every thing by prayer and supplication with thanksgiving let your requests be made known unto God.**

Prayer is simply talking with God in the name of Jesus. Living the Christian Life requires growing to spiritual maturity. One of the ways we grow spiritually is spending time talking with the supernatural God in the name of Jesus. When you pray, ask God in the name of Jesus to fill you with His Holy Spirit and to guide you through life. Ask Him to give you wisdom.

It was one of these times—when I was talking with God—that I received a supernatural message from God, and it was in the form of a dream. A couple at our home church had a little boy, but they wanted a little girl. In fact they wanted a little girl so bad that they had spent the past five years trying to adopt a baby girl. They had faithfully prayed and committed themselves to meeting every state requirement for adopting a baby to the point of tears. They were becoming discouraged, and it broke my heart!

I spent the next three months praying my heart out to God in the name of Jesus because I knew this was a very dedicated Christian couple, who came as a family to worship in the church. They never missed Sunday school and worship services, so I prayed during the night in the backyard for them to get a baby girl. At two in the morning, the soft moon light and stars set a grand mood. It was so quiet that you could almost hear the rabbits drinking water off of the grass!

I prayed for three months with my heart broken for this couple. The trees came in from both sides to form a canopy with a little room left to see the stars in the night sky. It was like the stained glass ceiling of a grand cathedral. I pleaded with God in the name of Jesus for them to be able to adopt a sweet baby girl. With tears I reasoned that there are many little girls that are orphans and many unwanted pregnancies and many little children that don't have a good Christian family.

So many baby girls need a family that loves them, but here are people I know for certain will raise their little girl to worship and serve God. And then one night, I had a dream from God!

In the dream, I was sitting on the couch with my eldest daughter, and we were looking through family photo albums. Pretty soon she asked me why there were no pictures of her in the family photo album. In the dream, I answered immediately "Because we don't have you yet."

When I woke up, I informed Sandy that God had showed me in a dream that we were going to have another baby and that it would be a girl. My wife had no reason to think she was pregnant and no thought that she would soon be pregnant, but nine months later, we had a baby girl.

I knew what the dream meant because God caused me to know it. Of course in real life, our couch was on the other side of the room; and in real life, she would be our youngest daughter. But that wasn't the point of the dream.

Three months after Joy was born, I had a serious problem: I had prayed my heart out for God to give the other couple a baby girl, but He gave *me* a baby girl. Oh no! I had to pray all the more. The thought was so unthinkable that I shared it with no other person. "God, do you want me to give them my little baby girl? I'm not sure I can do that . . . Oh God, please help me!"

I was in a lot of wonder and uncertainty. I didn't know what to do! The very next Sunday, the couple came to church all smiles and informed us that they were getting a new baby girl! I was so happy, and I learned a great principle about how God thinks and works. When we pray brokenheartedly with love and compassion for God to bless someone else without asking anything at all for ourselves, God will often bless us first.

If I had prayed for them while hoping I would also get a blessing too, it would have been a self-serving motive; and it would not be pure and holy before God. Such a selfish intention could not possibly be expected to be honored by the holy, pure, and perfect God.

Both our girl and theirs grew up together in church and in school. Both are now married, and both have little children of their own. Now it's thirty-four years later, and they still stay in touch and see each other from time to time. But the best part is that both of their families honor God, attend church, and teach their children about Jesus and His love. They teach their children to pray to God and help them grow in the wisdom and admiration of the God, who provided life and salvation to them!

# CHAPTER SEVEN

## God's Family!

### Visiting with Other Christians

As children of God, we are born again spiritually. We are now brothers and sisters in the family of God. Fellowship is visiting with other Christians in the family of God. Fellowship is absolutely essential to living a well-balanced and healthy Christian Life.

We are expected to love each other, pray for each other, and work together with each other to serve God. How can we love our brothers unless we get to know them? Together we can do more for the Lord than any one of us can do by ourselves.

> **1 John 4:21 And this commandment have we from Him, That he who loveth God love his brother also.**

> **1 Pet. 1:22 Seeing ye have purified your souls in obeying the truth through the Spirit unto unfeigned love of the brethren, see that ye love**

**one another with a pure
heart fervently . . .**

**Matt. 18:20 "For where two or three
are gathered together in
my name, there am I in the
midst of them."**

When God's people gather in the name of Jesus, He is there with them; and there is power when we agree in His name. As a new Christian, we will also learn many things from other, more experienced Christians. We need to come together regularly for love, fellowship, worshiping, learning, and praying with each other. Some people will say that you can be just as good a Christian at home as you can be at church, but that can never be true.

Just like logs piled up on a fire, the fire of the Spirit of God roars mightily when Christians join together to worship, pray, and share with each other in one accord. But if you lay a log over in the grass by itself, it will smolder, grow cold, and go out. Christians who go too long without coming together will grow cold in their spiritual excitement and tend to wander away into temptation and sin.

Select your church family wisely. Be careful to join a church that teaches the truth accurately from the Bible, God's Holy Word. Choose a church family of believers that demonstrate the love of Christ for others, both in the church family and for other people in the community around them. Join a local church congregation of believers actively involved in doing ministry and missions, not just studying about others doing ministry and missions.

**James 1:22 But be ye doers of the
Word, and not hearers only,
deceiving your own selves.**

It is also very hard not to bond with people you share food, fun, and worship with; but we need to share each other's pain too. Nobody should suffer alone. People need our comfort and prayers. Helping each other through a crisis also strengthens the family of God and draws us closer together with each other and closer together with God.

> **Heb. 10:24–25 And let us consider one another to provoke unto love and to good works: Not forsaking the assembling of ourselves together, as the manner of some is; but exhorting one another: and so much the more, as ye see the day approaching.**

Fellowship is sharing with other Christians. We learn, encourage, comfort, and pray for each other. We study the Bible, visit, and eat together. We are to love one another. Living the Christian Life requires growing to spiritual maturity. One of the ways we grow spiritually is in fellowship with other Christians.

We think of a family as a mother and a father living with their children. The family of God is the church. Christians become the children of God. We are all brothers and sisters through the blood of Jesus Christ. All truly saved Christians—of any race, color, culture, and language—are part of the same family of God through Jesus. The Spirit of God in us bears witness with the Spirit of God in our other brothers and sisters anywhere on earth and in heaven!

This is the Church family, and it includes all Christians who have gone on to heaven and those still here on earth. But each local congregation serves as the family of God here and now in the local community. Our Father is God through Jesus Christ; and Father God, Jesus, and the Holy Spirit of God are all in one. There is only one God, and He is our Father.

If you think of a local church congregation as a brick wall or concrete block wall or a stone wall, you will be able to understand and remember: every family and every person needs the nurture, love, and support of a family.

No person ever lived successfully on this earth without a support system! You will never make it by yourself, and nobody ever has. We should be very careful when building our support system and choose wisely what kind of people we associate with. You will eventually become like the people you spend time with. But trying to go through it alone is a big mistake.

A brick wall is the ultimate model of a support system, and it is an excellent tool to help you remember. Everywhere you go, you will see concrete block or brick walls to help you remember what a support system looks like. The basic concept is the same whether you use red bricks, yellow bricks, concrete blocks, or river stones to build the wall of your support system. Think of the Christian church as a family support system every time you see a brick or stone wall. The family of God is like the stone wall.

All of the bricks in the wall are laced together to support the bricks above. If you pull a brick or a stone out of the wall, it has no support system. Without its support system, the brick will fall—just like so many people and families have fallen. No matter how hard it tries, a brick cannot stay up by itself; and neither can you. By yourself, you will fail. But if we place the brick back into the wall, it can stay there for hundreds or thousands of years.

Of course we all know that you can't just start building a brick wall on top of the mud and the grass and the dirt. To build our family support system, we must first build a solid foundation for the support system to rest on. Just keep in mind that one of the bricks halfway up the wall represents you. All of the other blocks represent people and families in your support system.

Before you can surround yourself with people and families that believe as much as possible like yourself to build your support system, you first have to know what you believe in; then, you can select the kind of building blocks you will use. The foundation under your wall is your moral and ethical beliefs. The foundation of your support system is knowing what you believe is right and wrong.

Let's say someone asks you to get involved in some plan or questionable activity. You need to already have thought about what you will never do because you know it is wrong. You also need to know what you will always do because it is the right thing to do. If you don't have a strong moral and ethical belief system, you can be led astray by every bad person who is trying to use you to get what they want while getting you in trouble. But we aren't ready to install the foundation wall yet.

Before we can install the foundation for our family support system, we must first dig down below the freezing level and pour a solid footing for our foundation to be based on. Everything else in our life will be based on that footing. The footing under your foundation is your religious belief. Everything else rests squarely on this footing. Everything is based on your religious beliefs.

There cannot be any moral or ethical values without religion. Every person on the face of the earth has a religious belief even though many try to deny it or have never thought it through. Everything you believe in is based on your religious footing. The foundation wall of what you believe is right and wrong comes up from the footing upon which everything else is based.

Now that you have a firm foundation based on your religious beliefs, you can surround yourself with people that believe like yourself and build your family support system. Remember that people, men, women, and children above you in the wall of society depend on you for support as much as you depend on the bricks below you for support. That's a family—all helping each other to learn and to grow stronger. You can begin to surround yourself with people (men, women, and children of all ages) who share a common foundation with you. You look for people who believe as much like yourself as possible. This can be as simple as plugging into a church or congregation that is already preaching and teaching what you believe in.

Also remember that in today's world, there are more and more families that may include children without a daddy or a mommy. There are also single persons living all alone. It is the responsibility of all of our Christian brothers and sisters to include these and to help them complete their family support system.

Men in the church need to show the children what a Christian father looks like. Christian women in the church need to show the children what a Christian mother looks like. Even Christian children are a blessing to the older men and women who don't have children of their own. But in the local church, we all help each other to fill in the gaps. We help each other learn, worship together, pray together, grow together, and love each other with the love of Jesus.

Please note also that sooner or later, we will all be overwhelmed at some point in our lives by things we cannot deal with by ourselves. We might be overwhelmed by bills that we just can't pay, a death in the family, a painful family relationship or divorce, or the loss of children. At these challenging times, we will fail if we do not get help from our support system. At these times, it would be a big mistake to try to go through it alone.

Our church family can share our pain and concerns. Our church family can help us celebrate our successes. Our brothers and sisters can help us pray for God's wisdom, direction, courage, and strength. God's words in the Bible call this family the "brethren," which means brothers, and can sometimes be used to include all of the Christian women and children along with the men.

> **1 Tim. 5:1–2 Rebuke not an elder, but intreat him as a father; and the younger men as brethren; The elder women as mothers; the younger as sisters, with all purity.**

> **1 John 3:16 Hereby perceive we the love of God, because He laid down His life for us: and we ought to lay down our lives for the brethren.**

> **1 John 3:23-24 And this is His commandment, That we should believe on the name of His Son Jesus Christ, and love one another, as He gave us commandment. And he that keepeth His commandments dwelleth in Him, and He in him. And hereby we know that He abideth in us, by the Spirit which He hath given us.**

A young girl was asked by her grandmother why she always attended the certain local church. She pointed out that there are other churches in the area, so why did she choose this one? The young girl was quick and sure of her answer. She said "because they love me." Even children know if you truly care about them, and they will love you if you truly love them.

# CHAPTER EIGHT

## God Speaks!

### Study God's Words in the Bible

We know that if we don't eat, we will die. If a person doesn't put fuel in his/her vehicle, it won't run. The truth of God in the Holy Bible is our spiritual food. When living the supernatural Christian life, the truth of God in the Bible is our weapon against the wrong and evil of the devil. A steady diet of God's word is essential in knowing, understanding, and interacting with God the Father through Jesus the Son and the Holy Spirit.

The word of God holds all the secrets of life, success, and happiness. The Bible is the manufacturer's operation manual for the complex mankind that God created.

> **Luke 4:4 And Jesus answered him, saying, "It is written, That man shall not live by bread alone, but by every word of God."**

> **Matt. 4:4 But he answered and said, "It is written, Man shall not live by bread alone, but by every word that**

> **proceedeth out of the mouth of God."**

God speaks to people in many ways. God is all-powerful, and can do whatever He decides is best in any situation. We know of God speaking to people through angels, pastors, preachers, supernatural dreams, and visions. Sometimes people just know something came to them from God but don't know just how He did it. But the most reliable and accurate way God speaks to men, women, and children is through His words in the Holy Bible.

> **2 Tim. 3:16 All scripture is given by inspiration of God, and is profitable for doctrine, for reproof, for correction, for instruction in righteousness . . .**

Any dream, vision, message, or preaching that contradicts the Bible is not from God because the Bible is the only completely reliable source of absolute authority for the truth of God.

The Bible is God's own words, and God cannot contradict Himself! That is why no part of the Bible contradicts any other part of the Bible even though God used many different men over thousands of years as tools to put His words into writing for us.

> **1 Pet. 1:25 But the Word of the Lord endureth for ever. And this is the Word which by the gospel is preached unto you.**

> **Heb. 5:12–14 For when for the time ye ought to be teachers, ye have need that one teach you again which be the first principles of the oracles of God; and are**

**become such as have need
of milk, and not of strong
meat. For every one that
useth milk is unskilful in
the word of righteousness:
for he is a babe. But
strong meat belongeth to
them that are full of age,
even those who by reason
of use have their senses
exercised to discern both
good and evil.**

What a shame it would be if a baby did not grow and mature! But many Christians have not grown and matured because they do not know the words of God in the Bible. Sunday school classes, Bible study groups, and the preaching of the Good News of the gospel of Jesus Christ are some valuable ways we can learn more about God's Word.

But every Christian needs to get his/her own Bible so they can get into the habit of reading the Bible stories and studying the Bible. (A red letter Bible will show the words of Jesus in red.)

Bible study is learning from God's words in the Bible. We must know the scriptures because we must live by every word of God. Knowing God's word is essential to our healthy spiritual growth so we can live the Christian Life. One of the ways we grow spiritually is studying the Bible with the Holy Spirit's supernatural help.

Bible stories are exciting true-life stories that show how God, the Creator, deals with people. There are hundreds of adventurous true-life stories about how God deals with people in His Word.

Jesus also used parables to help people understand spiritual truths. The parable of the Good Samaritan, found in Luke 10:30–37, was a story Jesus used to help some people understand how to know who their neighbors were. A parable is not a true story but an illustration or word-picture story. A parable is story that is like a true situation that is likely to happen in a similar situation.

Parables are used as examples to help people understand a principle or truth. These parables are clearly labeled in the Bible so we can see which stories are illustrations and which are absolutely true-life accounts of historical events and miracles. A parable might start by saying "Heaven is like a certain man who . . ."

Remember not to miss your church's Bible studies, Sunday schools, worship, and fellowship times, wherein you can learn much more. Some exciting true-life Bible stories every Christian should know are listed below:

| | |
|---|---|
| God Created Heaven and Earth | Gen. 1 and 2 |
| How the First Man and Woman Became Sinful | Gen. 3 |
| Noah's Ark, The Great Flood, and Rainbows | Gen. 6:3–9:17 |
| The Tower of Babel | Gen. 11:1–9 |
| The Fiery Furnace | Dan. 3 |
| Daniel in the Lion's Den | Dan. 6 |
| The Birth of Jesus: The Christmas Story | Matt. 1:18–2:15 |
| Jesus Feeds 5,000 with 5 Loaves and 2 Fish | John 6:1–15 |
| The Death, Burial, and Resurrection of Jesus | Matt. 26, 27, and 28 |

But the Word of God is more than just history, more than just a spiritual guidebook: the Word of God is a supernatural power source!

Look at what happens when God speaks. When God speaks, cosmic forces respond to His will. When God speaks, He creates new truth. Even nature, science, and all of the rules of physics are forever changed as they obey His will.

On the first day of creation, God said "Let there be light." And the light began to shine even though the sun, moon, and stars weren't created until the fourth day! The words of God are powerful, and the Bible is the words of God! When we study God's words, we also are cosmically, miraculously, and forever changed. When we speak the words of God, the power of God's words pierce both the universe and the hearts of men with His supernatural and powerful truth.

> **Gen. 1:3–5 And God said, "Let there be light": and there was light. And God saw the light, that it was good: and God divided the light from**

the darkness. And God called the light Day, and the darkness He called Night. And the evening and the morning were the first day.

Gen. 1:16–19 And God made two great lights; the greater light to rule the day, and the lesser light to rule the night: He made the stars also. And God set them in the firmament of the heaven to give light upon the earth, And to rule over the day and over the night, and to divide the light from the darkness: and God saw that it was good. And the evening and the morning were the fourth day.

Rom. 1:16 For I am not ashamed of the gospel of Christ: for it is the power of God unto salvation to every one that believeth; to the Jew first, and also to the Greek.

Matt. 24:35 Heaven and earth shall pass away, but my words shall not pass away.

Isa. 40:8 The grass withereth, the flower fadeth: but the word of our God shall stand for ever.

Ps. 119:11 Thy word have I hid in mine heart, that I might not sin against thee.

Luke 4:4 And Jesus answered him, saying, "It is written, That man shall not live by bread alone, but by every word of God."

Mark 4:37–41 And there arose a great storm of wind, and the waves beat into the ship, so that it was now full. And He was in the hinder part of the ship, asleep on a pillow: and they awake Him, and say unto Him, "Master, carest thou not that we parish?" And He arose, and rebuked the wind, and said unto the sea, "Peace, be still." And the wind ceased, and there was a great calm. And He said unto them, "Why are ye so fearful? How is it that ye have no faith?" And they feared exceedingly, and said one to another, "What manner of man is this, that even the wind and the sea obey Him?"

Jesus says in John 14:13 "And whatsoever ye shall ask in my name, that will I do, that the Father may be glorified in the Son." So you can see that the words of God are powerful. Jesus is referred to as the Word that was made flesh, and He walked among us in the first chapter of

John. And this same chapter points out that Jesus is in fact the part of God that created heaven and earth in Gen. 1:1, long before He humbled Himself to return to us in the form of a baby born to a virgin—exactly as the prophets foretold more than 750 years before it happened.

But the Word of God is also powerful today when we speak it, read it, preach it, and believe it! The Bible is the divine, holy, accurate, and true Word of God; and it is the only reliable authority for what is true. The Word of God is alive. Jesus is risen from the grave, and He is alive. Jesus and the Word are not separate from each other. The Holy Bible is the written Word of God, and Jesus is the living Word of God; and He is fully human and fully God in His spiritual form.

By immersing yourself in the Word of God, you purify you heart. You can wash your physical body with water, but you wash your soul and heart with the Word of God.

> **Ps. 119:11 Thy word have I hid in mine heart, that I might not sin against thee.**

> **Eph. 5:26–27 That He might sanctify and cleanse it with the washing of water by the word, That He might present it to Himself a glorious church, not having spot, or wrinkle, or any such thing; but that it should be holy and without blemish.**

The Church is the bride of Christ, and the relationship between a husband and his wife is to be the same as that of Christ and the church. The head of the church is Jesus Christ.

We believe the Word of God is so important to the healthy, well-developed spiritual growth of children that we go every summer to teach Bible memory and the use of the Bible at Camp Cedar Crest. The children are given points for learning a verse well enough to recite it without looking at it. Level one is fifteen verses on a single sheet of paper.

Once level one is complete, a camper can advance to level two—somewhat similar to advancing through the levels of a video game. We require them to learn and recite the Bible reference at the end of the verse, as if the reference is part of the verse.

If a person doesn't know the location of the verse in the Bible, they will have serious problems trying to find it. The verses are carefully chosen and are the important verses leading to salvation and eternal life. For instance we ask them to say it like this:

> **"For all have sinned, and come short
> of the glory of God. Romans 3:23"**

> **"For the wages of sin is death; but
> the gift of God is eternal Life
> through Jesus Christ our Lord. Romans 6:23"**

> **"For God so loved the world, that
> He gave His only begotten Son,
> That whosoever believeth in Him
> Should not perish, but have
> Everlasting life. John 3:16"**

> **"Christ hath redeemed us from
> the curse of the law, being made
> a curse for us: for it is written,
> Cursed is every one that hangeth
> on a tree: Galatians 3:13"**

These are carefully selected basic Bible verses that will be used every day. These are the passages the children will hear being preached and discussed by the ministers, preachers, evangelists, missionaries, and teachers at their home churches. And level two is a page requiring them to learn to recite all of the books of the Bible in order!

Just think how hard it would be to look up a Bible verse if you didn't know what part of the Bible to look in. Level three is being able to look up any verse or chapter in God's holy Bible and find it in ten seconds or less! Levels four through twelve are mostly review and practice with a few new verses added.

Some children have special learning disabilities and work very hard just to recite one or two verses in a five–day Bible camp, but some are gifted or have some experience from their church or previous years in Bible camp and may complete all twelve levels. Of course, we have a wide variety of children that are somewhere in between.

Working with children with learning disabilities or kids with frustrations and distractions in their lives takes supernatural patience that only God can give! But we can never give up! How much is a child worth? The answer is "whatever it takes." God loves every one of them just as much as He loves us, and He has a wonderful plan for each and every life.

We keep stressing to the children that any person who learns even one verse of God's word is a winner; and the grand prize is knowing the words of God, which will help them through the rest of their lives.

Campers can build on what they have learned by attending Bible camp every year and by seeing the same material. What they learned the previous year will come back to them much faster, and each year, they will excel faster and be able to go farther. If a camper starts attending Bible camp at age eight, they will have nine years of experience and review by age sixteen!

As their Bible drill teacher, I have marveled each year at the progress the children have made in Bible skills, social skills, personal growth, and confidence. But it is the large stacks of Bible drill papers they turn in every year that brings tears to my eyes.

Last year my home church celebrated the salvation and baptism of campers following their return from Camp Cedar Crest, and I was asked to help baptize two other campers after camp at another church. One ten-year-old girl's mother also celebrated her own salvation—accepting Jesus as her savior, lord, and master—and was baptized with her daughter shortly following camp.

I heard a man comment that one of the girls he drove to camp was noticeably different and changed. He said the girl he carried home from camp was not the same as the girl he brought to camp. She acted more mature and more serious about God, worship, and prayer. He was excited, and so were the campers and parents he drove carpool for. It is very satisfying to know that lives are being changed and transformed by God's words.

# CHAPTER NINE

## Ambassadors for Christ

### Tell the Good News

If we know the truth, we must tell others. We cannot be a Christian without caring for others. We are to be examples for others. We must be the salt and light of the world, sharing truth and righteousness to all who will listen. We need to be Christ-like.

If Jesus is good and has love and compassion for others, then we, being His disciples and followers, too must do good and exercise love and compassion for others.

> **2 Cor. 5:19–20 To wit, that God was in Christ, reconciling the world unto himself, not imputing their trespasses unto them; and hath committed unto us the word of reconciliation. Now then we are ambassadors for Christ, as though God did beseech you by us: we pray you in Christ's stead, be ye reconciled to God.**

As ambassadors of Christ, we are to spread peace and good will; and we are to be responsible. We are the representation of God, not of ourselves. We come in the name of Jesus, not of ourselves. We should present ourselves in a professional and courteous manner. We must be people of honor and people that others respect, trust, and aspire to be like.

We should be known as people who build up and help others have a better life. God is good and His people build and bring life. The devil is evil and his people tear down, kill, and destroy. Evil spreads death and destruction while God gives life.

If a person says "God is merciful" but does not exercise God's mercy in dealing with other people, then they are not of God: they are liars. Our humanitarian concern for the good of others demands that we tell them about the love of God. This is one of the essential parts of growing spiritually mature.

We are called to be ambassadors for Christ. In early times, few people could read and write; and there was no radio, television, or newspapers! A messenger was sent to make announcements for the king or governor. Going from town to town, they would call out loudly or read "Hear ye, hear ye . . ." But why would anyone pay any attention? They did not represent themselves but someone far greater and more powerful than them. They would call out "By order of King George . . ." or "In The Name Of Caesar Augustus . . ." Like them, we also come representing someone far greater and far more powerful than ourselves: we come in the name of Jesus Christ.

Living the Christian Life means we must first be a Christian; but when we become a new Christian, we must grow spiritually. Christian maturity is a life-long, growing process. As we mentioned in chapter five, there are six essential things we must do to grow spiritually: prayer, fellowship, Bible study, witnessing, worship, and giving.

Being a witness is telling other people the Good News of Salvation and how to live forever. We must warn others that without Jesus, they have no hope of salvation.

**Rom. 10:13–15 For whosoever shall call upon the name of the Lord shall be saved. How then shall they call on**

**Him in whom they have not believed? And how shall they believe in him of whom they have not heard? And how shall they hear without a preacher? And how shall they preach, except they be sent? As it is written, How beautiful are the feet of them that preach the gospel of peace, and bring glad tidings of good things!**

It is our Christian duty to work together with other Christians to take the message of Jesus Christ and salvation through the cross to anyone who will listen. It is a life-giving message. In our own community, it is called witnessing and evangelism; but as we carry the message of Christ around the world, it is called missions.

It is the very message of life itself. Those who hear and believe will live forever in heaven, but those who try to get to heaven any other way will have no hope of Salvation! Only God has the right, the power, and the authority to make the rules; and God's word says that the only way is through faith in Jesus.

Anyone who rejects the only way God has provided will burn forever in the fires of Hell. Jesus is the only way to eternal life.

**John 14:6 Jesus saith unto him, "I am the way, the truth, and the life: no man cometh unto the father, but by me."**

If a policeman, soldier, or a restaurant worker wears a uniform, his every action is a reflection on the government or the corporation he or she represents. How should we dress? How should we conduct ourselves as Christians? Does our life show that we are different? Are we always a good model and image of Christ-likeness for others to follow?

An ambassador is an official representative and messenger of a king or ruler. He speaks on behalf of the king, and any disrespect towards the ambassador is an insult to the king and could result in a bloody war. We are Ambassadors for the Creator King and Ruler of Heaven and Earth!

No greater ruler or more powerful king than Jesus ever lived on the earth! We should certainly look and act in such a way as to gain the respect and honor of all we come in contact with. We are to be the visible example of what Christ is like. If we are faithful servants, God will back us up with His own power and authority.

How can we say we love people and demonstrate the mind of Christ unless we care enough to share the hope, meaning, direction, and purpose that Jesus brings into our lives? In God's Word, Jesus tells us to "Go and teach all nations."

> **Matt. 28:18–20 And Jesus came and spake unto them, saying, "All power is given unto me in heaven and in earth." Go ye therefore, and teach all nations, baptizing them in the name of the Father, and of the Son, and of the Holy Ghost: Teaching them to observe all things whatsoever I have commanded you: and, lo, I am with you always, even unto the end of the world. Amen."**

Jesus commanded us to do it and promises to go with us. Wouldn't it be hateful if we knew the bridge was washed out up ahead, and we didn't even try to stop the speeding car to warn the people? In the same way, we must warn people that without Jesus, they have no hope of salvation.

How can we say we love God and have made Jesus our master, if we don't love our friends and neighbors enough to share with them how they can know Jesus and have eternal life in Heaven? We need to be able to present the simple plan of salvation to the people with whom we go to school, work, ride the bus, or shop in the stores.

If you start by telling people they are lost and going to hell, they probably won't listen to you again; so it is better to begin by telling them that God loves them and cares about them. We can tell people that God has a wonderful plan for their lives. If we try to present the Good News of salvation, we are not responsible for people who choose not to accept the truth.

Witnessing is telling others about Jesus and how to have eternal life. Getting involved in missions, evangelism, and witnessing are essential for our healthy spiritual growth so we can live the Christian Life. One of the ways we grow spiritually is by telling others how to be saved.

# CHAPTER TEN

## In His Presence!

### Worship the Lord

One of the reasons God created man (meaning all people including men, women, and children of all race and gender) is for man to worship Him. When we come together to glorify, sing praises, and bow down humbly to worship the awesome God, who made us, we will feel His powerful presence with us.

Jesus has been made the King of Glory. He alone is worthy of our praise and worship. We must not neglect worship as it is one of our main reasons for being created. If we do not sing His praises, then how can we say that He is our Lord and Master?

How can we say that we love and serve the Lord if we don't praise and worship Him? He will not force us: He lets us choose, but He has opened His heart up to us and has held nothing back. He suffered more than any man ever can and died in our place on the cross. Surely we must open our hearts up to love and worship Him!

> **1 Chron. 16:29 Give unto the Lord the glory due unto His name: bring an offering, and come before Him: worship the Lord in the beauty of holiness.**

**Ps. 95:6 O come, let us worship and bow down: let us kneel before the Lord our maker.**

**Ps. 96:4–9 For the Lord is great, and greatly to be praised: He is to be feared above all gods. For all the gods of the nations are idols: but the Lord made the heavens. Honour and majesty are before Him: strength and beauty are His sanctuary. Give unto the Lord, O ye kindreds of the people, give unto the Lord glory and strength. Give unto the Lord the glory due unto His name: bring an offering, and come into His courts. O worship the Lord in the beauty of holiness: fear before Him, all the earth.**

What a grand and glorious privilege it is to worship the mighty God in His very presence! What a powerful feeling to know that the very creator of the earth and all that live desperately craves the honest and sincere praise and glory that we give! We must open our hearts all the way up to Him in total trust; and He will reach in and give us indescribable peace, joy, and confidence. He loves us and wants us to have the very best.

We can know for sure that if we give Him all that we have and are, He will bless it and multiply it to His purpose; and He will do what is the very best for us. Because of His powerful love and sacrifice for us, we can have total confidence and trust in Him.

**Rev. 4:11 "Thou art worthy, O Lord, to receive glory and honour and power: for thou hast created all things, and for thy pleasure they are and were created."**

Worship is humbly bowing down in the presence of the mighty king of the universe, glorifying and praising Him. One of the reasons God made us was so we could worship Him. One of the ways we grow spiritually is by worshiping God together in the name of Jesus.

# CHAPTER ELEVEN

*Your Mission*

## Called to Serve Him

Giving of yourself to minister to the needs of others means finding what God is calling you to do. Give from your heart. Because you care, you help others and support the ministry. You can give food or clothing to the poor or comfort people who are hurting. Of course money is also giving, and much needed.

Meeting the need may include giving kind words of encouragement or helping to build a new church. You may be needed to teach Bible stories to children, or maybe God has blessed you with the ability to play music or sing. God may have blessed you with extra food that you could share with a hungry family. If you grow flowers, maybe you could give some of them. Volunteers may be needed to help set up or take down tables and chairs.

In chapter 25 of the book of Matthew in the Bible, Jesus is telling the people a parable. A parable is a story to illustrate a truth. It is not the actual happening of a true story but is like a true story. A parable can be parallel to how something happened, happens, or will happen in the future. In Matt. 25: 31–46, Jesus is trying to help the people understand what His judgment will be like when He comes in His glory and sits on His throne in heaven as the King of glory.

**Matt. 25:37–40 "Then shall the righteous answer him, saying, "Lord, when saw we thee an hungered, and fed you? Or thirsty, and gave thee drink?" "When saw we thee a stranger, and took thee in? or naked, and clothed thee? Or "when saw we thee sick, or in prison, and came unto thee?" And the King shall answer and say unto them, "Verily I say unto you, Inasmuch as ye have done it unto one of the least of these my brethren, ye have done it unto me."**

Maybe you could take soup or tea to a sick person. Are you a good speaker? If God calls you to do something, He will help you prepare and do it. Meeting people's needs is a ministry of giving. All Christians are called to care and to help.

Giving is not just about money. Giving yourself to meet the needs of others doesn't always include money. Give your time and skills to help others. Giving is a valuable part of growing spiritually mature so we can live the Christian Life. Giving can include teaching, preparing or serving food, acts of kindness, and sweeping the floor. Is God calling you to preach, play music, help teach children, or mow the church yard?

In addition to the things God calls all Christians to do and to be a part of, we should also consider the possibility that God may be calling some of us to a full-time Christian ministry vocation. God may be leading you to prepare and study to serve as a pastor, preacher, evangelist, missionary, deacon, prison chaplain, truck-stop chaplain, Christian school teacher, or some other special calling.

Always keep in mind that there is not a more important or desperately needed calling than being a Christian parent, father, mother, grandparent, children's Sunday school or youth teacher. One of the most rewarding and vital things you can do for the Kingdom of Jesus Christ is helping raise the children to follow Christ, to learn about God, and to make a positive difference in the lives of children and youth. Among the smaller churches and rural areas, there is always a shortage of youth leaders.

Ask God in the name of Jesus to put you where He wants you to be and to show you His plan and will for your life. Ask Him to show you the work He is calling you to do and to give you the wisdom, strength, and courage to do it.

# CHAPTER TWELVE

## *Alone with God*

### In the Wilderness

When I retired after thirty years of employment under the State of Missouri, I finally had the opportunity to fulfil a lifelong dream. In the Bible, we are told by God about Jesus spending forty days in the wilderness. Again, we are told about Moses spending forty days on the mountain. There are always spiritual benefits from setting aside as much time as you can to focus on spending time alone with God.

Unfortunately I was only able to set aside two weeks for my time, which I call "Alone with God in the Wilderness. With a full retirement paycheck for the rest of my life guaranteed, I would never have to work again for money. I have since realized that it is far more fun and far more rewarding to work for free! It is especially pleasant and rewarding to work alongside other Christian volunteers who are also working for Jesus and not for money. We are now full-time volunteers.

> **Exod. 34:27–28 And the Lord said unto Moses, "Write thou these words: for after the tenor of these words I have made a covenant with thee and with Israel." And he was there with the Lord**

**forty days and forty nights; he did neither eat bread, nor drink water. And he wrote upon the tables the words of the covenant, the ten commandments.**

**Luke 4:1–2 And Jesus being full of the Holy Ghost returned from Jordan, and was led by the Spirit into the wilderness, Being forty days tempted of the devil. And in those days He did eat nothing: and when they were ended, He afterward hungered.**

It took many trips walking a mile and back to the truck for another load. I had to get the basic gear to the campsite. It was already late in the day on Monday, June 6, 2009. I had scouted out the location weeks before to find a secluded site in the Cedar Creek division of Mark Twain National Forest, not far from Guthrie, Missouri. I could see that evening was rapidly approaching, and I had no lights. It was also apparent that a heavy cloud cover would prevent any moon or starlight that night.

My purpose was to have some time alone with God. Away from the distractions of radio, television, games, entertainment, and telephones, a person can spend quality time with God. Man does not live by bread alone, but by every word that proceedeth out of the mouth of God.

We must learn to listen and to hear what God is saying to us. God speaks to us through His creation of nature, weather, and stars. God speaks to us through His words in the Bible. God speaks to us through other Christians. God speaks to men through angels, visions, dreams, and thoughts. Sometimes God's Spirit imparts to us understanding and truth even without our understanding how. This is a time of renewal and preparation to follow and serve God.

Although trying to hurry, I saw so many of God's wonderful creations—including turkey tracks in the soft mud, many deer tracks, and a nest of what looked a lot like white chicken eggs hidden tight up under a bush so close to the trail—that I wondered how I kept from stepping on them on my first trip in.

I only brought in what I felt was absolutely essential to set up for the first night. I would trek back to the truck to get additional supplies in the morning, but I really needed to rest. I was totally exhausted! I considered myself to be in fairly good health, but after three trips from the truck to the campsite in a hurry, I was concerned that I might be overtaxing my heart.

I estimated the site to be about a mile from the truck, so I had walked while lugging awkward and heavy gear about five miles; and the darkness of night was closing in. It would be too dark for another trip back to the truck.

Quickly stretching a strong rope between two trees, I stretched my tarp over the rope and made some makeshift tent pegs out of some nearby sticks, using some stout cord to tie down the corners of the tarp tightly. Overlapping several very large garbage bags on the ground to form a moisture barrier, I folded several blankets in half and stacked them up to form a cushioned bedroll; then I folded several sheets on top, leaving one unfolded sheet to cover up with.

I had selected this spot by carefully considering the distance from the nearest trees and the overhead clearance needed to build a safe campfire. I used the spade to dig a pit for the fire and surrounded it with large stones I found very close by—obviously used before by a previous camper to form a fire ring. I wondered how recently it might have been (or maybe it was over a hundred years?). This appears to be a very old forest with plenty of old fallen and rotting logs. I knew I would not have to go far to find plenty of firewood just lying on the ground ready to use. I had just slipped out of my outer pants and shirt and covered up with the top bed sheet when I heard it.

Off in the distance . . . Could I be hearing traffic on a distant highway or . . . No, that sounds like an airplane flying over—Oh no! That's thunder and it is getting closer. I know what I have to do.

In the privacy of the night, in a remote wilderness forest, it was just me and God. Barefoot and in my briefs and T-shirt, seeing flashes of lightning, I ran out and grabbed the spade and began to dig the trench along the top edge of the tarp tent.

I wanted the drainage ditch to be back under the edge of the tent so the water would run down on the outside of the trench and not get inside the tent. Any rain that fell short of the trench would run right inside the tent, soaking my bed and all of my supplies.

It seems to me like falling short is also a terrible thing mentioned in the Bible at Rom. 3:23! The trench must be deep enough to carry run-off water away from the high side, around the sides; and I wouldn't have to dig on the low side because all of the water would run downhill away from the tent.

I knew that if the water from the roof landed inside the trench, I would get very wet very fast. I was about halfway finished with the trench when the handle broke off the spade, but I couldn't stop now! I soon found out that the spade works just as well without the handle as it does with it. It was very much like my past memories of using an army trenching tool. Anyway, I couldn't stop now; the lightning was becoming more frequent, and the wind was beginning to stir things up. The thunder was very close now, and I began to feel some raindrops.

I quickly finished the trench so that it went all across the topside of the tent, around a tree, away from the tent, and down the hill. I moved everything that wasn't waterproof inside the tent. I set everything in a pile on the plastic bag floor, in the center of the tent or sealed it into huge suitcase-sized ziplock storage bags.

Once again crawling under the cover sheet, I was ready for bed; so now I prayed. After all, praying was one of the reasons I came out here to spend thirteen days alone in the wilderness with God. I was about to have my first very loud encounter with the powerful and mighty God, creator of heaven and earth and of nature and weather.

Even though I pride myself in being an experienced outdoorsman, I made a very serious mistake, which I would not be fully aware of until the next day and from which I would learn a very extremely painful lesson. I guess it had been a while since I had been able to find time to get away into the forest, leaving my skills a bit rusty. I'll tell you the painful lesson I learned later, but for now, let's just say it kept me humble.

God can speak to us in many ways. The fact is that God can speak to us any way that pleases Him. The question is not if, when, or how God will speak to us, but "are we listening?" Often I believe we miss what God is saying because we aren't listening. Well, God knows that, and tonight He decided to make Himself loud and clear! Here is my conversation with God the first night:

Suddenly the bright, stabbing, and booming voice of God resonated in extreme weather as God shook the very earth I lay on with the powerful exploding concussion that sounded and looked like lightning and thunder hitting the very tree I was lying under! All night God seemed to be saying "OK, John, "I know you are here. And I know you came to meet me here, so I'm letting you know that I'm here too! "And I'm powerful and I'm God and I am in control!" As the storm raged on into the night, I answered out loud; and the conversation went something like this as I prayed out loud in the name of Jesus. I said, "In the name of Jesus and by the blood of Jesus, "I hear you, God! "I know you are here. I know you are powerful, and I am not afraid because I know you are my protector. "I know you are testing my faith, and I am not intimidated because I know you love me, and I know you won't let anything happen to me. "I pray that you will help me get a good night's rest, and "I thank you for making yourself known."

I also knew that He knew I couldn't leave now—even if I wanted to—because God knew that with the pouring rain, the brook would be flooded; so a man on foot would be swept away. I also knew that God was aware that the only way I could get back to the truck was across an open field with bold and powerful lightning bolts crashing down around me!

There is no way to fully describe the awesome power of the sudden blinding flashes and earth-moving explosions and rumble when you seem to be right in the center of the target; you would just have to be there and experience it for yourself! All that night, the rain poured down; and the earsplitting thunder continued to sound like a war was going on just above the tent. The blinding lightning continued to light up the night all around me, and the wind blew.

I was glad for the coolness of the breeze, and it blew away any bugs that could have been a pest. I prayed for a while that He wouldn't let my tent blow away, and I would be sure to tie it down more securely tomorrow.

Although I was apparently in the very center of the earth-shattering thunder and powerful lightning, I was asleep very shortly and slept soundly. I was completely dry and had already been alone with God in the wilderness in a very dramatic way on the very first night! This is a very good start to a promising two weeks in a remote part of the National Forest with God.

During the night, the rain put the fire out, soaking the ashes to the very bottom of the fire pit and leaving me in total darkness, except for the flashes of lightning. All firewood is soaking wet with no chance of drying out any time today. It is now Tuesday morning; and the humidity is very high, leaving clothing somewhat damp.

The brook is still flooded, but the rain has stopped. My socks and shoes are sopping wet from walking in the tall, wet grass along the trail; but I must go very early into town because I am beginning to realize the very serious and painful mistake I made the night before!

I could feel the muscles of my thighs tightening and the muscles beginning to cramp. I realized I was in dire danger of experiencing one of my severe and extremely painful "Charley horse cramps. If that happened, I knew the pain would be totally debilitating; and I had not brought the necessary V8 juice and Gatorade I knew was needed to prevent or treat the painful cramps.

The mere memory of such severe pain from the past was enough to make me want to cry. I drank some water as I knew that would help some. Through the night, I had overtaxed my thigh muscles because my bed was turned the wrong way. Lying across the gentle slope had caused me to use my leg muscles all night to keep from rolling down hill, out of bed, and out of the tarp I call a tent. I must turn my bed so that my head is straight uphill, and my feet are directly downhill. This way I will not be lying across the slope, so I can fully relax the leg muscles.

I reasoned that if anyone came to visit me in the forest, they would wait till later when things dried out some, and the flood in the brook receded; so I went into town very early so I could hurry back. Once in town, I took a shower and got fresh socks and an extra pair of dry shoes. I also grabbed a flashlight. I would walk the mile back into the campsite barefoot and carry the shoes in a plastic bag from now on to keep them dry. (I hate wet socks and shoes!)

I brought back enough of the small V8 cans to drink one every night at bedtime and drink some water with it, some calcium and vitamin D tablets, and enough small Gatorades to drink one at about 2:00 p.m. for the remaining twelve days. I brought back charcoal and lighter fluid and soon had a rip-snorting fire burning. I also kept several jugs of drinking water on hand at all times.

Although it rained some today, I was able to read some today in Isaiah, roast a sweet potato in the coals of the fire, and meet face-to-face with a delicate yellow butterfly. I was sitting in a lawn chair, writing some notes from my Bible studies on a yellow legal pad and reading in the book of Isaiah.

After the sun came out and things began to dry some, several bright yellow butterflies came fluttering around. One of them came and landed on the top edge of the tablet while I was still writing. It showed no fear, and I got a really close look at its face. Now I have experienced, up close and personal, both the most big and powerful storm and the most delicate little yellow butterfly of God's creation.

A butterfly's face is a curious sight to behold! Instead of lips that go across the face like those on people and animals, a butterfly's mouth is a really long vertical slot where a chin should be all the way up to about two-thirds to the top of their head. From the vertical slot thrust a really long tongue, reaching down to probe around on the yellow paper. I suppose the butterfly could be tasting to see if the colored paper was sweet like a yellow flower? I remember thinking that the butterfly and the legal pad paper were almost exactly of the same color.

This was to be a day of rest and healing. I will also be sure to keep my socks and shoes dry. I also made sure to tie down the tent more securely as you never know when another storm may come, and I promised God last night that if He would protect my tent from blowing away, I would tie it down more securely during the daylight hours when it wasn't raining. I left about a six-inch space between the edge of the tarp and the ground to allow air to blow through, and both ends were completely open.

During the entire two weeks, I never got cold and never used more than one sheet to cover up. Some nights I asked God (always speaking with God in the name of Jesus) if He could send a little more breeze, and sometimes He did.

Two Christian cowgirls came riding their horses into camp one day. A mother and her daughter came by on horseback to visit briefly but didn't have much time. They are members of the Capital Region Cowboys for Christ and live nearby. They didn't get down from their horses; but we read a Bible passage and prayed together, which was simply talking with God in the name of Jesus, before they had to leave again. I was very thankful for their support and for the effort they made to come.

The mother is getting two copies of the award-winning book *Hope Rising* to give to some patients she works with. I am considering giving copies of the book as Christmas gifts to some very special people this year. The book is a series of short stories about how God uses some very special horses to provide love and understanding for neglected and abused children. The second day has been very eventful, and I will not allow the fire to go completely out for the next eleven days. I also observed that night comes thirty minutes to an hour earlier in the dense woods than out on the open fields nearby.

Well it's a new day, and I am still physically tired but spiritually energized as I am still expecting great things from my time alone with God. I often talk out loud as I speak to God in the name of Jesus. I am ever mindful that as I learn how to listen with supernatural discernment, the Holy Spirit will help me listen to hear God speaking to me. I believe God is always talking to us, but we often miss out on what He is saying because we aren't focused on paying attention.

In this modern time, there are ever-increasing distractions from spending time with God. Between employment and sleeping, we try to squeeze in time to eat, read, study, browse e-mails, exercise, play video games, see movies, and spend time with our families and friends.

There is very little time to be alone with God. God should come first, and then everything else will work out better! God speaks to us through His word, nature, weather, other Christians, dreams, and visions, (sometimes) in an audible voice, and in any other way He chooses.

His dealing with each person is different and personally tailored to your own needs. I want to be tuned in and not miss this special opportunity. I know I cannot get forty days alone in today's fast-paced world, but I am very thankful for the thirteen days I have.

I'm pretty sure my system is getting too low on protein because I feel tired and weak. Today I read about some of the times when Daniel and Moses spent time alone with God and look into some of the special visions they were given by God. I'm thinking "wouldn't that be great if it happened to me?" I know that God can do that, but if He does, it won't be to make me feel prideful or better than anyone else: it would be to fulfill His purposes and bring glory and honor to Him, not me.

I have also been wanting to study more about the end-of-time prophecies from the Bible without the influence of other preachers and teachers. Sometimes people can possibly be incorrect in their understanding of "end-time prophecies. I find it is always best to look for myself to see what God's word says and not just accept everything someone is preaching and teaching.

My socks and shoes are drying by the fire while I read in the Bible. I really hate wet socks and shoes and find that I would prefer to walk barefoot in the wet grass than to wear wet socks and shoes—something a type-two diabetic is warned never to do. I hear the turkey hens today and again almost every day but will not see any during the entire two weeks.

I didn't venture out of the campsite very often during the day. I found that the nighttime dew makes the tall grass so wet that walking out of the dense forest and into the open field before 11:00 a.m. makes you dripping wet all the way above your knees. In the afternoons, the heat and humidity is very uncomfortable, damp, and clingy.

Even though I had envisioned this trip to include some walking along the numerous forest trails, most days I just stay in the comfort of the dense woods. Here it was dryer in the mornings and felt fifteen degrees cooler in the afternoons. Who would have thought that two weeks in late June would be so hot? As it turns out, we had several colder nights later in the middle of July.

By this time, I was fighting an all-out war with ticks. I saw very few mosquitos during the entire time but was constantly pulling off ticks. These little brown central Missouri ticks seem to be more of an inconvenience than a real danger. Most of the disease-carrying ticks seem to be in other areas. I finally learned to use more insect repellent—and to use it more effectively.

If you spray your feet and shoes up to your ankle and on any socks you are wearing and roll your pantlegs down and spray all the way up to your knees, then that is good for about eight hours. You also need to spray your hands wet, and rub it on your face, neck, and the back of your neck. You also need to rub it in the hair on the top of your head, but be careful not to get it in your eyes. I learned that a partial or half-hearted approach doesn't work with ticks any better than it does with spiritual matters!

I won the war with the ticks. As a result, I pulled off about twenty-seven ticks during the first week but almost none the last week. After it was good and dark, I was pretty sure nobody would come to visit; so I hiked to the truck and drove over to Moser's grocery in Holts Summit to get some protein. I found a very fresh-looking KC strip that looked to be about a half-inch thick. I also picked up two citronella candle bowls so I could burn one inside on one end of the tent at night. I felt like it would help keep insects and animals away and give me a little light at night.

I was fully aware that a trucker ran over a mountain lion over on Highway 54 about eight miles east from here a few years ago and reasoned that there could still be some in the forest somewhere. Coyotes can sound really spooky at night although they are harmless. But I also heard what might be a pack of dogs nearby, and wild dogs could be a problem if they came upon a man who was fast asleep. I talked to God almost every night about putting my total faith in His protection while I was asleep and pretty much helpless at night.

I always claimed victory in every situation in the name of Jesus and by the blood of the cross. I know God will never fail. I'll leave the KC strip in the original foam package inside of a plastic shopping bag, inside a waterproof ziplock bag; and I'll cover it up with gear on the floor of the tent to keep it cooler. I'll cook it tomorrow, but tonight I will eat a six-inch subway sandwich I picked up in Holts Summit, Missouri.

I was still pretty tired on Thursday, so I slept a lot during the day as well as at night. And it was a good thing I did too because wow! After a rainy and wet first three days, I suddenly realized the sky is completely clear. This could be the special night! Anticipation is building, and I already know God is here.

I already know that if I came specifically to spend time alone with God, my daddy (Father God) would make sure this was a special time together for us. With all the time out here, I expect God to do something new and special; and I'm pretty sure I know what is coming, but I never expected it to be as good or as dramatic as it was about to turn out! I had a long talk with God and told him what I was thinking.

I made sure the iron skillet was good and hot first; then I laid the KC strip on the hot skillet, and it hissed. I left it there just briefly to make sure the surface was sealed. This is a pure, fresh, lean cut of beef. Don't add salt or seasoning of any kind until after the steak is cooked all the way through. Now use the metal spatula to turn it over and seal up the other side. ***Hishshssss!*** Now I pull the skillet over to a reduced heat and let it cook more slowly until I'm pretty sure it is fully cooked at least halfway through.

Just thinking about how it smells makes my tongue water all over again. "Thank you, Jesus, for this time together and the beauty of the best protein ever cooked. "Thank you for the clear sky. "Your vast creation is powerful evidence of your power! "It would be wonderful to have a crystal-clear night way out here with no lights to take away from the beauty of your moon, stars, constellations, and planets tonight. "I would be so grateful, God, for a clear view of your handiwork. "Thank you in the name of Jesus."

Now I turn my steak over and cook the other side slowly until I'm confident the meat is done all the way through. Now you need to move very fast! Really good steak must be served immediately. Do not overcook or let the steak cool because any steak that is reheated will never be as good.

Now I sprinkle just a pinch of iodized salt over the steak, turn it over and sprinkle a pinch of sea salt over the other side. Quick! Take it up from the cast-iron skillet, and put it on the plate. Now you can see the juice welling up and oozing out. That's why you don't want any seasoning or salt until it's done: if the salt draws all of the juice out while it's cooking, it will get tough. From the very first bite . . . "Oh yes, no fancy restaurant in the world can top this!

It was already late in the day when the two Christian cowboys came walking into camp. The two brothers walked up the trail past my campsite then followed the smell of smoke from my campfire back through the woods. I knew them from Capital Region Cowboys for Christ. We sat around the campfire, and I was thankful for their visit. These two brothers are solid in their faith and know God's word. They were a great support and encouraged me in my quest to spend time with God.

They encouraged me and prayed to God for me to seek His guidance and wisdom in following His will for my life in retirement. They prayed for the Holy Spirit to lead my wife, Sandy, and me as we seek to do His will in our new ministry. It was completely dark when the two cowboys left. Although I offered them a flashlight, they assured me they would find their way just fine. After a circle of prayer, they faded into the night along the trail. And now it is time!

I took a new tarp—clean and dry—and carried it out into the grassy field. Seeking an area with a clear view of the magnificent heavens, I stretched it out. The grass, most of it taller than my chest, was already soaking wet; but the tarp would keep me dry, and the pressed-down grass under the tarp formed a very comfortable cushion. Lying on my back, I had a grand view of the sparkling ceiling of God's magnificent heavens on a cloudless night.

> **Ps. 33:6 By the word of the Lord were the heavens made; and all the host of them by the breath of His mouth.**

> **Heb. 1:10 "And, Thou, Lord, in the beginning hast laid the foundation of the earth; and the heavens are the works of thine hands. . . ."**

> **Ps. 19:1 The heavens declare the glory of God; and the firmament sheweth His handywork.**

As I was looking up into the crystal ceiling of God's natural cathedral, the choir began to sing! That's right! As I marveled at the great power of God displayed in the magnificent heavens on a cloudless night, the tree frogs were singing, not at random but in unison—a sort of rhythm like they were a huge choir; then the bullfrogs chimed in and sang the bass part, and it was all so beautiful. There was no moon out tonight, so not even the glow of the moon could detract from the dramatic and spectacular star show tonight. It would be early tomorrow morning before the moon would be out, and the planets would line up; but I didn't have a telescope.

I saw lots of blinking airplane lights go by during the next two hours and a couple of satellites. They all seemed to be so far away like they were part of the fantastic display of stars and planets rather than being a distraction. I slept rather well that night but woke up around 3:30

a.m. to go out and view the moon and the larger planets that were not visible the night before.

The exact days and dates seem to run together in my memory after that, and I probably should have kept a more detailed journal record; but many special events stick out in my mind. I remember one day, I heated some water on the fire and took a warm bath; but early the next morning while walking along the trail, I couldn't resist the freshness of the little brook as it flowed crystal clear.

I reasoned that I had total privacy because it was very early in the morning. (There was barely any daylight, so it was maybe 5:30 a.m.?) It was also right on the tail end of a heavy rain, and few people ever use this trail. Surely nobody would be out this early on a rainy morning. With the hot muggy weather, the running water was so clear and looked so cool. And besides all that, there was a long, square stone with just the right height—like a bench for my clothes—so I took a cool, refreshing bath in the stream. It was wonderful!

I remember looking at the same pool again the next week with disgust. After many days without God's life-giving rain, it was a stagnant pool of scum and bugs. It was not clean at all! I remember thinking that after several days away from God's life-giving Bible study, prayer, fellowship, worship, witnessing, and giving, we all get kind of spiritually stagnant and nasty.

I learned a few curious things about Whip-poor-wills too! A Whip-poor-will is a favorite bird to hear on camping trips in June and July in Missouri. Often their call is heard in late afternoon or at dusk. Well, I got serenaded quite a lot. I don't know if it was the same bird each time or a different one, but I observed that they have a ritual method to their calling. I'd never listened to one so close above me in the perfect quiet of the national forest. I found the experience kind of weird and mysterious.

First, a Whip-poor-will has to wind up almost like a mechanical device or a robot! They start low and make a whirring sound as if they are pumping up a flywheel. You can hear each whirring sound getting a pitch higher until they get up to the note they will sing; then they begin to sing. "Whip poor will" they say in their high-pitched whistle. The word "whip" is sung then "poor" in a slightly lower note; then the word "will" is in a much higher pitch, and they hold it longer. This is where they get their name Whip-poor-will from, but they run the words together as if it was one word. They do, however, change the pitch of the note on each word so that it sounds like a phrase of three distinct words or syllables.

They always repeat the phrase several times, but this is the most mysterious part: when you are up close and personal, you can hear a soft mechanical clicking sound between every word. So it goes like this: The bird, which you almost never see but only hear, starts winding up, starting low and building up. **Weer-er-er-er-er-er.** Once they wind up, they don't have to wind up again until they wind down.

They sing "Whippoorwill"—click—"Whippoorwill"—click— "whippoorwill." The click is very soft and is slipped in between calls so quickly that it is usually not heard unless the bird is very close, and you are listening for the click. Now if the bird stops singing, it is not through yet and may sing again in a few minutes, but normally it will not fly over to another tree or quit singing until it unwinds first, progressively starting high and spiraling down. **Weer-er-er-errr.** Once the bird winds down and flies to another tree, it has to wind up again to sing again.

One night a raccoon came and stole an apple by cutting the bottom out of a plastic bag. The next night, I made some bread in the iron skillet and left it out for the coon, and he came and ate it. The third night, the raccoon brought a friend with him to eat skillet bread; and I got a picture, but the picture was pretty dark.

Altogether I would say that my time alone with God in the wilderness was exciting. It helped me grow and learn a lot about God, prayer, nature, and listening to hear what God is saying. I also think God enjoyed spending time with me and teaching me things I had never experienced before. I encourage everyone to spend some time alone with God, and if you can, go camping or fishing with Him.

Everyone needs to set some time aside to talk with God, engage in fellowship with other Christians, study God's Word, look for ways to tell and show others about Jesus, worship and praise the mighty God in the name of Jesus, and minister to the needs of other people—both saved and those who do not have salvation yet.

# CHAPTER THIRTEEN

## Exercise Faith

### Fully Trust Him

Faith is believing. Faith is knowing in your heart that something is true and dependable. Faith is believing and not giving up. If you trust in God with all your heart, He will never let you down.

> **Heb. 11:1 Now faith is the substance of things hoped for, the evidence of things not seen.**

> **Matt. 21:22 "And all things, whatsoever ye shall ask in prayer, believing, ye shall receive."**

Without faith, you cannot be saved! You must believe in Jesus Christ with all of your heart. While we are saved by grace, which is a free gift despite the fact that we don't deserve it, we are only saved if we believe. Even though we are saved by grace, it is activated by faith. See what God's Word says. Watch for the word "faith" in these two passages from the Holy Bible.

> **Eph. 2:8–9 For by grace are ye saved through faith; and that not of yourselves: it is the**

**gift of God: Not of works,
lest any man should boast.**

**Gal. 3:13–14 Christ hath redeemed us
from the curse of the law,
being made a curse for us:
for it is written, Cursed is
every one that hangeth on
a tree: That the blessing of
Abraham might come on
the Gentiles through Jesus
Christ; that we might
receive the promise of the
Spirit through faith.**

When I was nine years old, I prayed. I repeated my prayer often and from time to time. I had a serious rash on my legs as far back as I can remember. At nine years old, I had no memory of ever being without the itching, scratching, and scabs on my legs. All those in my family felt sorry for me, but I learned to live life and to go on. I didn't think about it all of the time. I didn't feel anyone should feel sorry for me or treat me any differently. I just focused on other things.

I remember once when I spent some time with my aunt and uncle and cousins in rural Illinois. After sleeping in the bed all night, my aunt said it looked like someone had sprinkled cereal on the bed from the scabs I had scratched off during the night. She also reported that there were traces of blood on the bed sheets.

Later I heard about Job in the Bible scratching his sores with a piece of broken pottery, and I knew exactly what he was doing as I had used the edge of a knife to scrape the sores that itched on my legs.

**Job 2:8 And he took him a potsherd
to scrape himself withal;
and he sat down among
the ashes.**

At the age of nine years old, I prayed to God in the name of Jesus, asking Him to heal my legs and to make them as healthy as any other person's legs. I went ahead and thanked Him in advance for healing them. I also told God that I believed He was already healing them even if I couldn't see any progress yet.

I repeated the same prayer many times over the next four years, but I never doubted that God was doing what He thought best; then one day, when I was thirteen years old, God showed a team of doctors at the University of Missouri how to cure the disease.

We were given a small silver tube of white cream to rub into the wounds and were instructed to wrap them up in saran wrap and to only unwrap them when going to sleep at night. The end result was completely normal legs with no sign of scars that I can see.

Since that time, I have thanked God many times for His healing. But the point is that we must put our faith in God and trust in Him no matter what. We must trust in God even when we don't see any results. We must have faith, and we wouldn't have the opportunity to practice our faith if every result was immediate.

I do not believe in unanswered prayer. I believe we sometimes just don't want to accept God's answer. I believe that if we put our prayers and needs in the hands of the supernatural God of the universe in the name of Jesus and trust in Him unfailingly, we are absolutely guaranteed to have victory in every situation with no exceptions.

I believe God will do what is best for everyone involved, but it may not be always what we expect or want. In the Bible, the words faith and belief are the same as used in a sentence. Being faithful means that your faith endures forever and that your actions show evidence of your unwavering belief and trust in God forever. Those who are faithful until the end do not live like a Christian one day and like the devil another day.

> **Rom. 5:1 Therefore being justified by faith, we have peace with God through our Lord Jesus Christ . . .**

> **Phil. 3:9 And be found in Him, not having mine own righteousness, which is of the law, but that which is**

**through the faith of Christ,
the righteousness which is
of God by faith . . .**

True faith is believing with all your heart no matter what. True faith endures the test of time. True faith means unfailing trust and believing over the long haul. Faithfulness is enduring until the end. The Lord endures forever. True faith must include patience and endurance without end. And your actions must show your faith in God. You must believe and never give up believing. Faithfulness is forever.

> **James 1:3–4 Knowing this, that the trying of your faith worketh patience. But let patience have her perfect work, that ye may be perfect and entire, wanting nothing.**

And in closing, I repeat: everyone needs to talk with God, engage in fellowship with other Christians, study God's word, tell others about Jesus, worship and praise the mighty God in the name of Jesus, and minister to the needs of other people.

And remember to practice the six words of Action that lead to Christian growth and Maturity:

1) Prayer        (talking with God in the name of Jesus)
2) Fellowship    (sharing with other Christians)
3) Bible Study   (learning from God's Word)
4) Witnessing    (telling others about Jesus)
5) Worship       (praising & glorifying God in Jesus' name)
6) Giving        (giving of yourself for the needs of others)

And these need to be done continuously. How long would a person live without food? How long would a person live without drinking water? How long would a person live without breathing? And how long would a person stay strong and healthy without spiritually breathing and eating the Word of God?

See that you do not neglect any of the six, and continue to grow spiritually. It is your duty as a Christian to learn all you can and to teach it to as many as will listen so that they too may be able to live the Christian Life.

"Go ye therefore, and teach all nations."

CPSIA information can be obtained at www.ICGtesting.com
Printed in the USA
LVOW06s1052160415

434744LV00002B/118/P

9 781503 537071